CALGARY PUBLIC LIBRARY
NOVEMBER 2019

ADVENTURES ON
EARTH

SIMON TYLER

PAVILION

First published in the United Kingdom in 2019 by
Pavilion Children's Books
43 Great Ormond Street
London
WC1N 3HZ

An imprint of Pavilion Books Company Limited

Publisher and editor: Neil Dunnicliffe
Assistant editor: Harriet Grylls
Art director and designer: Lee-May Lim

ISBN: 9781843654278

A CIP catalogue record for this book is available from the British Library.

10 9 8 7 6 5 4 3 2 1

Reproduction by Mission Production Ltd., Hong Kong
Printed in China

This book can be ordered directly from the publisher online at www.pavilionbooks.com, or try your local bookstore.

TABLE OF CONTENTS

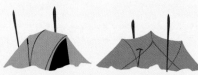

INTRODUCTION

Welcome to the amazing world of exploration

The wild places of our planet have always fascinated and amazed—from the soaring, snow-capped peaks of the Himalayas to the tumultuous raging oceans that separate the great continents of the world. Over the centuries, great adventurers have explored these places and returned home with fascinating tales to tell.

Navigators have sailed across the oceans, discovering new lands. Travelers have traversed deserts and jungles, establishing routes and rediscovering the remains of ancient civilizations. Mountaineers have conquered the highest and most difficult peaks, and polar explorers have reached the most northerly and southerly points of the globe.

Vinson Massif

The Ellsworth Mountains is a large mountain range situated in Antarctica. It is home to Mount Vinson—the highest mountain on the Antarctic continent at 16,050 feet.

This book explores the wild places of our planet, and the great adventures that have taken place while people have explored them. In the following pages, we will visit the polar regions, mountains, volcanoes, oceans, rivers, deserts, jungles, forests, and cave systems deep underground. We will hear about the pioneering adventurers who first explored these places, use maps to learn about the routes they took, and meet some of the local wildlife along the way. In parts of this book, you may find some scientific or geographical terms that you are unfamiliar with. The first time these are used they are highlighted in CAPITALS, and all of these words and phrases are explained in the glossary at the end of the book.

THE POLAR REGIONS

The areas on Earth surrounding the POLES—the two points around which our planet spins—are known as the polar regions. These fall within the highest and lowest CIRCLES OF LATITUDE, more commonly known as the ARCTIC CIRCLE and the ANTARCTIC CIRCLE.

These regions are really cold, because the light and heat they receive from the sun arrives at a low angle and therefore spread out, meaning the surface of these regions receives less heat than other parts of Earth. There is also complete darkness for much of the winter in these regions. The length of this dark season increases as you move closer to the poles. At the poles themselves, the dark season lasts six months.

Humans have long inhabited the outer fringes of the Arctic, with PALEO-ESKIMO peoples now known to have lived in the region more than 4,000 years ago. Exploration in the Arctic has a long history.

The Antarctic was never natively inhabited, and it was first viewed by humans only in the nineteenth century. Exploration followed, and today many nations maintain research stations on the continent of Antarctica.

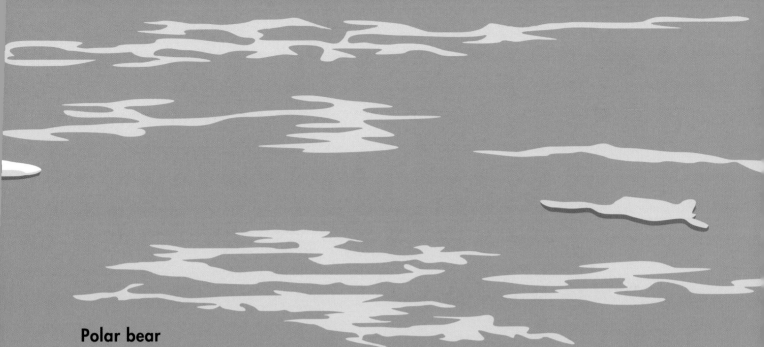

Polar bear
Ursus maritimus

Dependent on the sea ice of the Arctic region, polar bears are marine mammals, well-adapted to their cold environment. They have large feet that help them to swim and to spread their weight when they walk on snow and thin ice. Bumpy pads on their paws help them grip onto icy slopes. They have a thick, fatty layer under their fur, which keeps them warm at low temperatures. They are known as hypercarnivores, because more than 70 percent of their diet is meat—mostly seals, which they hunt for at the edges of sea ice sheets.

The polar bear is classified as a vulnerable species on account of the risks to their habitat posed by the shrinking of the Arctic ice cap, caused by climate change.

ALASKA

RUSSIA

CANADA

ARCTIC CIRCLE

Beaufort
Sea

Chukchi
Sea

1962 British
Trans-Arctic
Expedition route

Laptev
Sea

Arctic
Ocean

Kara
Sea

NORTH POLE

FRANZ
JOSEF
LAND

GREENLAND

SVALBARD

Greenland
Sea

Norwegian
Sea

ICELAND

NORWAY

FINLAND

SWEDEN

North
Sea

GREAT
BRITAIN

THE ARCTIC

The Arctic is a region surrounding the North Pole. The Arctic Circle is the line of latitude that runs approximately 66 degrees north of the equator.

Unlike its Antarctic cousin, the Arctic is not a continent. Most of the ice sheet that comprises the area surrounding the North Pole is the frozen surface of the Arctic Ocean. The land areas that surround the ice cap include sections of the most northerly parts of North America, Europe, and Asia. The approximate size of the Arctic ice cap is shown in pale blue on the map on the left. Every summer, its edges break up and float away as icebergs, and every winter the seawater around its edges freezes, trapping floating ice chunks into a continuous ice sheet.

Humans have lived within the Arctic Circle for many years. From the earliest Paleo-Eskimo to the later Thule and Inuit, these hardy indigenous peoples have learned to live in the extreme cold, perfecting techniques for hunting marine animals, such as seals, walrus, and whales, and land animals, including polar bears and caribou. There are around 150,000 Inuit still living in Arctic Greenland, Canada, and Alaska.

Human explorers have long been drawn to the wilds of the Arctic. Many expeditions to the North Pole were undertaken in the late nineteenth and early twentieth centuries. A number of these claimed to have reached the pole, but these efforts are now disputed. The first verified journey to the North Pole was achieved by Roald Amundsen and Umberto Nobile in the airship *Norge*, on May 12, 1926. They flew over it without landing. A Russian scientific expedition, led by Aleksandr Kuznetsov, landed three Lisunov Li-2 airplanes at the pole on April 23, 1948, and was the first confirmed team to stand at the pole itself.

The Arctic environment is under threat because of GLOBAL WARMING. Human industrial activity around the world releases chemicals known as GREENHOUSE GASES into the air. These are so named because they cause the atmosphere to warm up like a greenhouse. This effect means that the average temperature around the world is increasing and, as it does so, the area of the Arctic that remains frozen is shrinking every year. One direct effect of this is that ice that previously remained trapped in the Arctic is gradually flowing away into the oceans. Like pouring extra water into your bathtub, the level of the seas around the world is now increasing, which affects human and animal populations living in low-lying coastal areas.

Arctic tern
Sterna paradisaea

An amazingly well-traveled seabird, the Arctic tern spends the northern summer months breeding in colonies along the coasts surrounding the Arctic Ocean, from Alaska and Canada to northern Europe and Russia. It then migrates south to escape the Arctic winter, sometimes traveling as far as South Africa, Australia, and even the northern parts of Antarctica. Arctic terns regularly cover more than 43,500 miles in a year, and go on to travel more than 1.25 million miles over their 30-year lifespan.

The species is carnivorous. They generally feed on small fish, crabs, and krill, as well as insects while on land during the breeding season.

THE NORTH POLE ON FOOT

Walter "Wally" Herbert was a British polar adventurer who led one of the most audacious expeditions ever undertaken. An experienced Antarctic explorer, Wally Herbert spent six years meticulously planning a journey across the Arctic Ocean. This journey was to be completed on foot with dog teams to help pull the heavy sleds full of equipment and supplies. Before the expedition, Herbert organized four months of training in northern Greenland, during which time he learned dog driving techniques from the Inuit, and covered 1,500 miles from Greenland to Canada.

The Trans-Arctic Expedition consisted of glaciologist Roy "Fritz" Koerner, SAS medic Ken Hedges, experienced polar explorer Allan Gill, and Herbert himself (shown left to right below, with one of the giant sleds), as well as 40 husky dogs.

The team set off from Point Barrow, Alaska, on February 21, 1968. Each man was responsible for a heavy sled and a team of dogs.

By July, the ice was breaking up in the warmer conditions, so they erected a camp to sit out the summer months. At this point, they had already traveled 1,180 miles. They resumed their journey in February 1969, by which time the average temperature had dropped to −40 degrees Fahrenheit.

Battling these fierce conditions through the Arctic winter, they finally reached the North Pole on April 6, 1969. Their supplies were already running short and, by the time they reached the end of their crossing, they were severely malnourished. They arrived at the Svalbard archipelago on May 29, 1969, having completed a journey that had taken 463 days and covered an incredible distance of more than 3,725 miles.

Wally Herbert's Trans-Arctic Expedition was the first to reach the North Pole on foot, and the first (and last) expedition to cross the ice-covered Arctic Ocean on foot.

During the expedition, Fritz Koerner made a series of scientific investigations into the nature of the Arctic sea ice. Donning a wet suit and diving into the cold ocean (below), Koerner measured the thickness and characteristics of the ice sheet. His efforts resulted in the first detailed survey of the nature of Arctic ice, and this went on to play an important role in assessing the effects of climate change. For example, since he recorded his data, the average thickness of the ice has become thinner and thinner.

Atlantic Ocean

King Kaajan VII Sea

Weddell Sea

Brunt Ice Shelf

⑫

⑬

⑭

Larsen Ice Shelf

⑮

⑲

⑱

⑯

⑰

Ronne Ice Shelf

1955-58 Commonwealth Trans-Antarctic Expedition route

Bellinghausen Sea

SOUTH POLE

①

Vinson Massif

Research Bases

1—Amundsen-Scott (United States)
2—Vostok (Russia)
3—Concordia (Italy/France)
4—Scott—New Zealand
5—Mario Zucchelli (Italy)
6—Dumont d'Urville (France)
7—Casey (Australia)
8—Mirny (Russia)
9—Mawson (Australia)
10—Syowa (Japan)
11—Dome Fuji (Japan)
12—Maitri (India)
13—Troll (Norway)
14—Kohnen (Germany)
15—Halley (Great Britain)
16—Dan Martin (Argentina)
17—Rothera (Great Britain)
18—Vernadsky (Ukraine)
19—Palmer (United States)

Transantarctic Mountains

Amundsen Sea

⑪

Ross Ice Shelf

④

1911-12 Amundsen Expedition route

1911-12 Scott Terra Nova Expedition route

Bay of Whales

⑤

Pacific Ocean

Ross Sea

THE ANTARCTIC

The Antarctic is a region surrounding the South Pole. The Antarctic Circle is the line of latitude approximately 66 degrees south of the equator.

Antarctica is a mountainous continent covered in ice. The Antarctic ice sheet is particularly thick, reaching a depth of 15,750 feet in the east section of the continent. This vast sheet of ice holds 61 percent of all fresh water on Earth.

Antarctica has never had indigenous peoples living on it, but today it is home to many scientists, who live at research stations scattered around the coasts and inland.

Captain Cook's Second Expedition crossed the Antarctic Circle in 1773, but treacherous ice floes prevented them from reaching the coast. The First Russian Antarctic Expedition made it to within about 18½ miles of the continent in 1820. The first confirmed landing on Antarctica was made by the crew of the Swedish-Norwegian whaling ship *Antarctic* in 1895.

Amery Ice Shelf

West Ice Shelf

Davis Sea

Shackleton Ice Shelf

Mawson Sea

Emperor penguin
Aptenodytes forsteri

Unique to the continent of Antarctica, the emperor penguin is the largest and heaviest penguin species on Earth. This hardy bird breeds during the freezing cold of the Antarctic winter and, once their chicks hatch, the mother and father take turns to undertake lengthy foraging journeys, returning with bellies full of fish, squid, and krill. They then regurgitate some of this food to feed the growing chick.

Like many other species living in the polar regions, the emperor penguin is endangered because of the effects of climate change.

Indian
Ocean

AMUNDSEN AND THE SOUTH POLE

Roald Amundsen was a Norwegian explorer who led the first successful expedition to the South Pole. He was born in 1873 in the village of Borge. His family was a seafaring one, but his mother made him promise to break from tradition and go to school to become a physician. When Roald was in his early twenties his mother died, and he gave up medicine to pursue his dream of becoming an explorer.

His first expedition was as a first mate on the Belgian Antarctic Expedition between 1897 and 1899. The team was the first to spend an entire winter on the continent of Antarctica. Between 1910 and 1912, he focused his attention on the South Pole. He and the other members of his team—Olav Olavson Bjaaland, Hilmer Hanssen, Sverre Hassel, and Oscar Wisting—constructed a camp—Framheim Base—at the Bay of Whales on the Great Ice Barrier. From here, they organized their equipment and sled dogs, then ventured inland to lay store depots containing food and fuel.

After an aborted attempt in September 1911 due to bad weather, he set out again with his team the following month. Their dangerous journey took them across the Ross Ice Shelf, beyond which they discovered a glacier that gave them passage onto the high Antarctic Plateau. They named the glacier Axel Heiberg after a Norwegian who had funded early polar expeditions. The glacier was a fortuitous discovery, because without it the climb up to the plateau would have involved ascending the precipitous Transantarctic Mountains. The Norwegians were well-skilled both at skiing and driving their dog-pulled sleds, and they were able to travel fast and efficiently across the Antarctic ice. They reached the South Pole at 3 p.m. on Friday, December 14, 1911.

Amundsen and his team returned to Framheim, following snow cairns they had left to help them retrace their route (cairns are trail markers normally made by piling up stones). The descent of the glacier was enjoyable for those on skis, but for the men driving the heavy, hard-to-control sleds, this section of the journey was filled with danger, because the glacier was littered with deep crevasses. Once back on the Ross Ice Shelf, they accessed their supply depots, and made it back to Framheim by January 25, 1912. Their journey had taken 99 days, and they had covered about 2,140 miles.

Their jubilation was short-lived. Their competitors—Robert Scott and his Terra Nova Expedition—successfully reached the pole 34 days after Amundsen's team, but they succumbed to frostbite and exhaustion on their return journey. Scott and his four companions perished.

CROSSING THE ANTARCTIC

Between 1955 and 1958, an expedition led by Englishman Sir Vivian Fuchs became the first to successfully traverse the continent of Antarctica via the South Pole. The Commonwealth Trans-Antarctic Expedition was the first to reach the pole by land since the Amundsen and Scott expeditions 46 years previously, and the crossing of Antarctica overland would not be repeated until 1981.

Before the expedition began in earnest, Fuchs journeyed to Antarctica to set up a base camp—Shackleton Base—at Vahsel Bay on the Weddell Sea coast. This was achieved, although their vessel *Theron* became stuck in the ice and was badly damaged. Fuchs returned to London, leaving a team to construct the camp huts and organize dog teams and vehicles. The Antarctic winter conditions were savage, and wind and blizzards hampered their work. They also lost some supplies when the ice shelf they were being stored on broke off and drifted out to sea.

Fuchs and the other members of the team sailed back, and together they finished the work at Shackleton as well as constructed another South Ice Base 300 miles closer to the pole. After the following winter, the team set off on their journey. They traveled using three Tucker Sno-Cats, two Studebaker Weasel tracked vehicles, and a Bombadier Muskeg tractor.

At the same time, the New Zealander Edmund Hillary set up another camp—Scott Base—on the opposite side of the continent, and then began to create a series of supply drops between there and the South Pole. Hillary pressed on to the pole, where the American Amundsen-Scott South Pole Station had been established. Fuchs met Hillary's team at the pole, and then continued onward to Scott Base. The Antarctic crossing was a journey of 2,158 miles and took the team 99 days to complete.

Tucker Sno-Cat

Built in Oregon, the Tucker Sno-Cat was a vehicle developed for telephone-line maintenance during North American winters. Even so, the three used in the expedition required many modifications for the more extreme conditions of the Antarctic continent. The engines were specially prepared to run at really low temperatures. The bodyworks were checked and sealed to prevent ingress of snow and icy winds, and the interiors were lagged with thick, synthetic insulating material in an effort to keep the occupants warm.

LIVING IN ANTARCTICA

Halley VI Research Station
Brunt Ice Shelf

The British Antarctic Survey's Halley VI Research Station is a state-of-the-art scientific facility that performs a range of research activities, including investigating climate change, rising sea-levels, and space. In 1985, data collected at Halley led to the discovery of holes in the Earth's ozone layer as a result of atmospheric pollution. The current Station is modular—the eight modules that make up the base are mounted on hydraulic ski legs, and the entire base can be divided and then towed to a new position. This is necessary as the ice shelf it sits on constantly moves towards the Weddell Sea, and breaks up. The station was transported to a safer site in the winter of 2016–17.

As you can see from the map on pages 12–13, there are research bases scattered all over the continent of Antarctica. These range from the huge US Amundsen-Scott South Pole Station, which houses up to 150 personnel, to smaller stations such as Russia's Vostok, which hosts around 12 scientists. Life in the Antarctic can be tough. Scientists prepare by completing safety and survival courses before they depart for the continent. They are also issued with specialised cold weather clothing to keep them warm during their time on the ice.

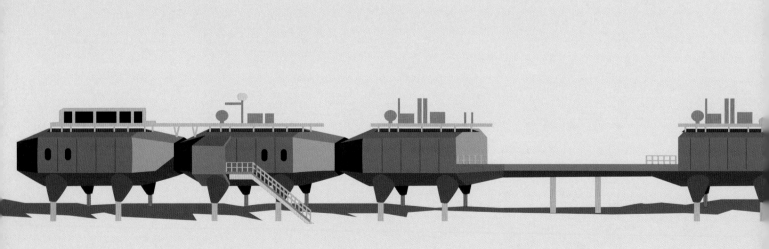

Personnel on the large research stations enjoy a tasty and varied diet thanks to teams of chefs working in well-stocked kitchens. Those living on the smaller stations and in tents conducting fieldwork must endure a more rudimentary menu, made up of mainly freeze-dried and tinned food. Antarctic personnel generally sleep in shared bedrooms or dormitories, which are heated and well-insulated. They often have access to a small gym, communications equipment (so they can chat with their families via Skype), and sometimes even a sauna!

The most challenging season is the winter, during which the temperatures at the Halley Station remain below -4 degrees Fahrenheit, and often drop as low as -13 degrees Fahrenheit. This is compounded by a 105 day period of total darkness when the sun doesn't rise. Venturing outside during this period is especially dangerous, though scientists are sometimes rewarded with spectacular views of the Aurora Australis, also known as the Southern Lights.

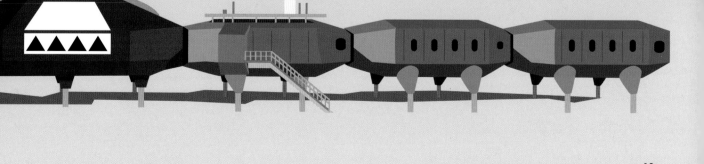

THE MOUNTAINS

Mountains are found throughout the world, from the frozen continent of Antarctica to volcanic island chains in the Pacific Ocean. The peaks of the highest mountains are cold, desolate places, but at lower elevations the mountain environment is often home to a diverse selection of animals and plants that have adapted to the less hospitable climatic conditions. Human society also exists at surprisingly high altitudes in the mountains.

Throughout history, many mountains have been revered as sacred places, because their height positions them closer to the heavens. The ancient Greeks believed Mount Olympus was the home of the gods. Many Hindus believe that Mount Kailash in Tibet is the home of the god Shiva.

Mountains have also long been a target for adventurers. High-altitude mountaineering is now popular, with many guided ascents of the highest mountains taking place every year. However, it remains a dangerous endeavor on account of strong and unpredictable mountainsstorms and the debilitating effects of altitude.

DENALI
ALASKA
Height: 20,310 feet

Denali is the highest mountain in the continent of North America.

It is located in the Alaska Range, which is the most northerly section of the Cordillera mountain chain that runs down the backbone of the American continent.

BROOKS RANGE

ALASKA
RANGE

THE ROCKIES

2

SIERRA MADRE
OCCIDENTAL

THE ANDES

3

ATLAS MOU

MOUNTAIN RANGES AROUND THE WORLD

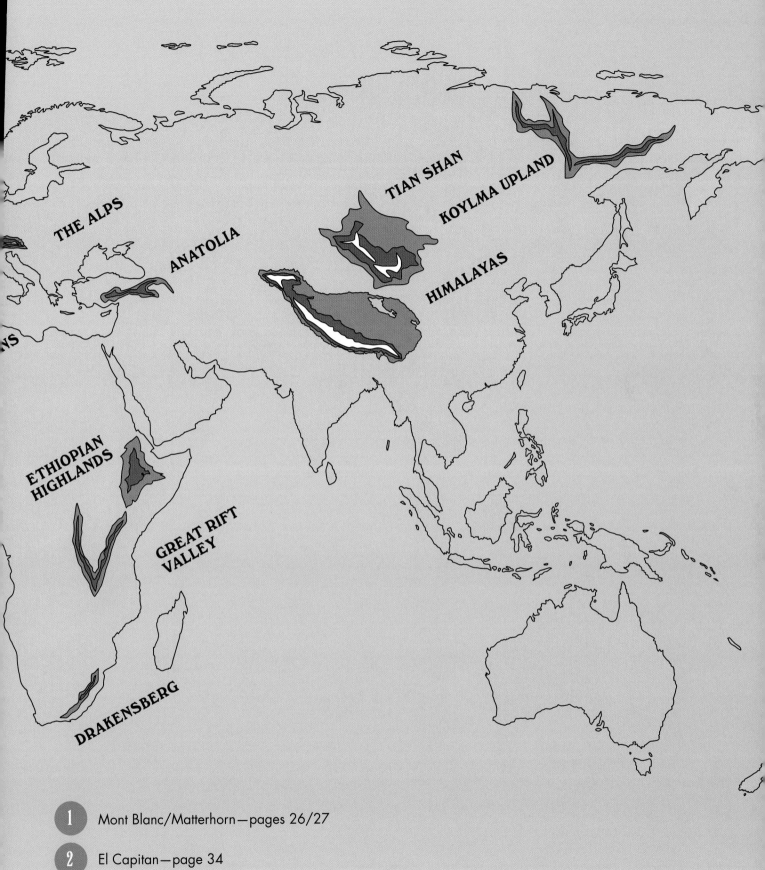

THE ALPS

ANATOLIA

TIAN SHAN

KOYLMA UPLAND

HIMALAYAS

NS

ETHIOPIAN
HIGHLANDS

GREAT RIFT
VALLEY

DRAKENSBERG

See page 24 for Himalayan peaks.

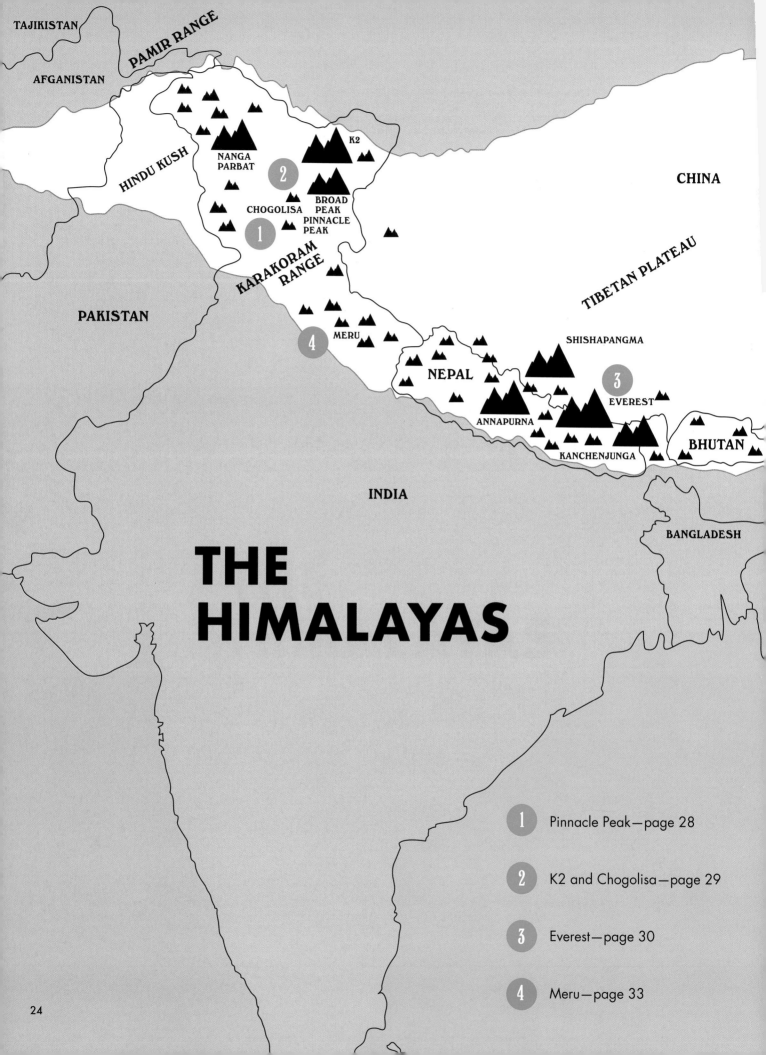

TAJIKISTAN

PAMIR RANGE

AFGANISTAN

HINDU KUSH

NANGA
PARBAT

K2

CHINA

CHOGOLISA

BROAD
PEAK

PINNACLE
PEAK

KARAKORAM
RANGE

TIBETAN PLATEAU

PAKISTAN

MERU

SHISHAPANGMA

NEPAL

EVEREST

ANNAPURNA

BHUTAN

KANCHENJUNGA

INDIA

BANGLADESH

THE HIMALAYAS

The Himalayan range is home to the greatest mountains on Earth. Stretching across southern China, the whole of Nepal, and the northern reaches of Pakistan and India, its peaks soar to heights up to more than 29,000 feet.

The name Himalaya is Sanskrit and means "abode of snow." Many peoples have made the Himalayan foothills their home, including the Nepalese Sherpas, the Hunza people of northern Pakistan, and the Tibetan people, now living in the Chinese Tibet Autonomous Region.

As well as forming the source of some of the greatest rivers—the Ganges, Indus, and Tsangpo-Brahmaputra—the Himalayas are home to a diverse variety of wildlife. In the uplands below the snow line, forests of rhododendron, birch, and juniper provide habitats for the snow leopard, ibex, and the Tibetan wolf. Bearded vultures, griffon vultures, and golden eagles circle in the skies above.

The Himalayan mountains have played host to some of the most daring and dangerous exploits in the history of mountaineering, and they continue to offer incredibly hard challenges to the most talented climbers.

Yak
Bos grunniens

The domesticated yak is a large, heavily built animal that is related to the domesticated cow. They are well-adapted to life in the high mountains, having evolved a large, powerful heart and capacious lungs.

In the Himalayan countries of Nepal and China, yaks are used as pack animals, to transport goods over high mountain passes. Their milk is used to make cheese and butter. Yak butter is used to make tea in Tibet, known as po cha.

EARLY MOUNTAIN ADVENTURES

Mountain climbing as a recreational activity originated in Europe in the eighteenth century. The period of European history known as the Enlightenment saw a rise in popularity of outdoor pursuits, appreciation of the wonders of the natural world, and of recreational exploration. The range of mountains known as the Alps is the largest in Europe, and this became a focus for the early mountaineers, or alpinists as they became known.

MONT BLANC—1786
Jacques Balmat and Michel-Gabriel Paccard

Mont Blanc is the tallest peak in western Europe, standing at a height of 15,781 feet. It was the obvious target for mountaineers, but its steep icy flanks repelled many attempts. The effects of altitude contributed to the difficulty. In 1782, Jacques Balmat, a mountain guide, and Michel-Gabriel Paccard, a doctor and scientist—both from the town of Chamonix, which sits at the base of the mountain on the French side—made the first successful ascent. Equipped with little more than warm clothing and steel-tipped walking sticks, they forged a route up Mont Blanc that their rivals had dismissed as impossible. In doing so, they won both plaudits and awards. They laid the foundations for the future pursuit of high-altitude mountaineering.

MATTERHORN—1865
Edward Whymper

One of the most iconic mountains in the world, the pyrimidal peak of the Matterhorn is situated on the border of Switzerland and Italy. Unlike many of the larger Alpine peaks, it is rocky and precipitous on all sides. Many talented mountaineers attempted the mountain, but it was not until 1865 that a team managed to reach the summit.

An English illustrator, Edward Whymper had already made many attempts on the mountain. Eventually, along with his companions Francis Douglas, Charles Hudson, and Douglas Hadow, one French guide, and two local Swiss guides, Whymper discovered a route up the Hörnli Ridge that led the team to the top.

During the descent Douglas Hadow, who was a novice climber with much less experience than the others, slipped on the ice and knocked over the French guide, Michel Croz. Croz and Hadow began to slide down the steep slope, pulling Francis Douglas and Charles Hudson with them. The rope snapped, leaving Whymper and the Swiss guides standing on the slope. The other four all plunged to their deaths.

EARLY CLIMBS IN THE HIMALAYAS

PINNACLE PEAK
1906

The American mountaineer and explorer Fanny Bullock Workman learned to climb on the rocky outcrops of New Hampshire in the late nineteenth century. Later, she and her husband, William Hunter Workman, embarked on lengthy bicycle tours across Europe and then North Africa and India. During the latter trip, they visited the Karakoram Himalaya. They subsequently made this the focus of their future exploratory endeavors, returning to the region eight times.

In 1906, at the age of 47, Fanny made the first successful ascent of Pinnacle Peak, a 22,740-foot mountain in the Zanskar region. In doing so, she set an altitude record for female mountaineers and, on her return, won numerous awards for her achievement. She climbed with great conviction and purpose, and she was able to operate at high altitudes without too much problems from altitude sickness. She later explored the Hispar and Biafo glaciers via the Hispar Pass, becoming the first woman to traverse any Himalayan glacier (let alone two) and proving her ability on dangerous and unpredictable terrain.

K2 and CHOGOLISA
1909

Prince Luigi Amedeo, the Duke of the Abruzzi, was an Italian nobleman who led some of the most ambitious mountain and polar expeditions ever undertaken. His greatest expedition was to the highest mountains of the Karakoram Range.

They first tackled K2 (also known as "The Savage Mountain" because of how difficult it is to climb). They chose to attempt the southeast ridge of the mountain, with their base camp on the Godwin-Austen glacier. Despite relatively primitive equipment, they reached about 20,500 feet, and the ridge is now known as the Abruzzi Spur.

They then diverted their attention to Chogolisa, another mountain to the south. They were about only 560 feet from the summit before they had to retreat due to bad weather. The height they reached—24,600 feet—was a new high altitude record, which remained unbroken until the 1922 British Mount Everest Expedition.

MOUNT EVEREST

HILLARY STEP

NUPTSE

LHOTSE

SOUTH COL

WESTERN CWM

KHUMBU
ICEFALL

EXPEDITION FACTS

The 1953 Everest Expedition team was made up of 15 mountaineers, accompanied by 362 porters. Their equipment, although cutting edge at the time, was extremely basic by today's standards. Their oxygen tanks were heavy, unwieldy, and unreliable. The radios that they used to communicate between camps were bulky, and the batteries didn't last long in the cold conditions.

CONQUERING EVEREST

The first ascent of Everest was one of the greatest achievements in the history of exploration. The expedition was planned by the Royal Geographical Society and the Alpine Club, and was led by Colonel John Hunt.

1 BASE CAMP—17,900 feet
The team made camp below the Khumbu Icefall—a dangerous region of steep, glacial ice full of deep crevasses. Finding a route through this would be essential to allow the expedition access to the higher slopes of the mountain.

2 CAMP TWO—19,400 feet
An intermediate camp at the side of the icefall. From here the climbers could see their route beyond this part of the mountain, and the legions of Sherpas began to carry equipment and supplies up to Base Camp.

3 CAMP THREE—20,200 feet
Once the route through the icefall was complete, the climbers could concentrate on forging a path up the steeper, higher reaches of the Western Cwm, while the teams of Sherpas began to resupply Camps Two and Three.

4 CAMP FOUR—21,000 feet
Once the route through the icefall was complete, the climbers could concentrate on forging a path up the steeper, higher reaches of Everest, while the teams of Sherpas began to resupply Camps Two and Three.

5 CAMP FIVE– 22,000 feet
6 CAMP SIX—23,000 feet
7 CAMP SEVEN—24,000 feet
Camp Five was situated on the lower section of the face of Lhotse. The following two camps were higher on the Lhotse face. The climbing was steep and unrelenting here. The climbers were also experiencing the debilitating effects of the altitude, and they had to make repeated trips back down the mountain to recover.

8 CAMP EIGHT—26,000 feet
The route up the Lhotse face gave the climbers access to the South Col— a narrow yet level area between the summits of Everest and Lhotse. This would be the base for the final summit push. On May 26, 1953, the team of Charles Evans and Tom Bourdillon set out for the top. They reached the south summit at 28,700 feet, but had to turn back because of exhaustion and problems with their oxygen tanks. The following day, Edmund Hillary and Sherpa Tenzing Norgay left on their bid for the summit.

9 CAMP NINE—27,900 feet
Hillary and Tenzing spent a perilous night in a tiny tent at Camp Nine— high up on the southeast ridge.

S SUMMIT—29,029 feet
Hillary and Tenzing managed to ascent a particularly steep section of rock that guarded the final section of the mountain. This rockface is now known as the Hillary Step. The climbers reached the summit of Everest at 11:30 a.m. on May 29, 1953.

31

MERU PEAK AND THE SHARK'S FIN

Situated high in the Garhwal Himalaya in northern India, Meru is a precipitous mountain with extremely steep flanks. Because of its vertical nature, it is a difficult mountain to climb. It has three peaks—North, Central, and South. The hardest Central Peak was first climbed by the Russian mountaineer Valery Babanov in 2006. His line up the mountain is known as the Shangri-La route.

An alternate route up the Central Peak follows a high blade of rock known as the Shark's Fin, because of its distinctive shape. The Shark's Fin route is one of the hardest high-altitude climbs in the world. It involves much of the difficulty of the hardest sections of El Capitan or Cerro Torre, but at much higher altitudes and with stronger, unpredictable weather. The upper sections of rock overhang steeply, and the climbing is precarious and hard. First attempted in the 1990s, the route repelled team after team of exceptionally talented climbers until an American team made it their goal.

Conrad Anker, Jimmy Chin, and Renan Ozturk first attempted the Shark's Fin in 2008. They reached a point only 500 feet below the summit, but they were forced to retreat when storms battered the mountain. They sheltered from the storm inside their portaledge tent, hanging off the side of the Fin.

Returning in 2011, they made a successful ascent of the mountain during a prolonged spell of clear weather. Their ascent was lauded as one of the greatest in the history of mountaineering, and the achievement was even more impressive, because Renan Ozturk had experienced a serious brain injury during a skiing accident only five months prior to the expedition.

Shangri-La route

The Shark's Fin route

EL CAPITAN

The magnificent granite monolith of El Capitan (Spanish for "The Captain") is situated in Yosemite National Park, California. Rising more than 3,600 feet above the pine and fir trees at the valley floor, it has been at the forefront of exploratory rock climbing since the 1950s. Its hardest routes remain at the cutting edge to this day.

The first ascent up the face of El Capitan followed the prominent center line—The Nose— and was completed in 1958 by Warren Harding, Wayne Merry, and an assortment of other climbers. It was a long siege ascent taking 45 days—the steepness of the face made progress slow, and the team spent many days on the face, camping on ledges and in hammocks. The first ascent of The Nose in a day was completed by Jim Bridwell, John Long, and Billy Westbay in 1975. Since then, speed climbing The Nose has become a challenge for top climbers, and the record as of 2019 is 1 hour 58 minutes 7 seconds.

Most ascents of The Nose involve aid climbing—pulling up on metal bolts and climbing equipment inserted into cracks in the rock. The first free-climbing ascent—pulling up using only the rock itself—was achieved by the top American climber Lynn Hill in 1993.

The Salathé Wall lies to the left of The Nose, and it was first free-climbed by Americans Todd Skinner and Paul Piana in 1988. The German Huber brothers established a variation called Freerider a decade later. On June 3, 2017 the American rock climber Alex Honnold climbed Freerider solo—without any rope or protective equipment—making this the first free solo climb of El Capitan.

To the right of the Nose lies a blank section of the face known as the Dawn Wall. This was thought to be impossible to climb without using aid techniques. However, in January 2015, Americans Tommy Caldwell and Kevin Jorgeson made the first free ascent. They spent 19 days on the face. The route is the hardest on El Capitan—and one of the hardest anywhere in the world.

Size comparison
Left to right:
Eiffel Tower, Paris, France—1,063 feet
Empire State Building, New York—1,454 feet
The Shard, London, England—1,016 feet

Below:
The Nose, El Capitan—2,900 feet

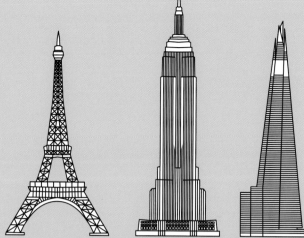

Freerider Route

The Nose Route

The Dawn Wall Route

CERRO TORRE

The Compressor Route

Situated in Patagonia, in an area of the southern Andes between Chile and Argentina, lies a huge icefield, the second largest on Earth outside the polar regions. Through this ice, incredibly steep granite mountains poke up, topped with overhanging, mushroom-shape snowfields. Cerro Torre is the tallest of one particularly steep group. It rises to 10,262 feet, with a face of 4,026 feet above the icefield below.

The Italian mountaineer Cesare Maestri claimed to have climbed Cerro Torre in 1958. However, the climbing community distrusted Maestri's account of his exploits. Maestri returned in 1970 with a gas-powered compressor drill, which he used to place metal bolts up the southeast face. He did not climb the final icy section at the top, instead leaving the compressor tied up at the top of the rockface and abseiling down.

In 1974, an Italian team of Daniele Chiappa, Mario Conti, Casimiro Ferrari, and Pino Negri climbed to the summit of Cerro Torre for the first time. In 1979, El Capitan legend Jim Bridwell and Steve Brewer repeated what is now called the Compressor Route (shown in pink, left), continuing up the icy section above to the summit. In 2012 Americans Hayden Kennedy and Jason Kruk climbed Cerro Torre without using any of Maestri's bolts, and removed 125 of them on their way down in the spirit of partly returning the mountain to its natural state.

Andean Condor
Vultur gryphus

Found in the Andes and along the west coast of South America, the Andean condor is one of the largest birds in the world. Its wingspan is easily more than 10 feet.

It scavenges on the carcasses of dead llamas, alpacas, deer, and cattle. In ancient Andean culture, the condor was the symbol of the sun god.

VOLCANOES

Potent symbols of the power of the Earth's geological forces, volcanoes are gigantic structures formed by ruptures in our planet's surface. The Earth is formed of huge and, importantly, separate sections, known as TECTONIC PLATES. Below the plates lies ferociously hot molten rock, known as MAGMA. When the plates move together or apart, the divisions between them become volcanically active, and the immense pressure inside the Earth pushes the magma upwards. When it breaks through the crust and reaches the surface it becomes known as LAVA. During this process existing volcanoes erupt, and sometimes new volcanoes are formed.

Volcanoes get their name from Vulcan—the Roman god of fire. The Romans named a Mediterranean island—Vulcano—after him. They believed that this fiery-top mountain was the chimney of Vulcan's subterranean workshop, and that the regular earthquakes in the region were the shocks caused by him hammering weapons for the other gods. Other peoples around the world hold religious and mythical beliefs about volcanoes, including the native Mexican Nahuas, who believe that Popacatapetl was a grieving warrior who was turned into an an angry "smoking mountain" by the gods.

Because of the immense dangers of possible eruptions, volcano exploration and science (known as volcanology) is filled with risk. As well as explosions and hot lava flows, volcanoes release toxic gases that can overwhelm humans within minutes unless they are well-prepared with breathing equipment. They can also produce devastating mixtures of gases and rock fragments known as PYROCLASTIC FLOWS, which sweep down a volcano's slopes at high speeds, obliterating trees, buildings, and people in their path. The Roman cities of Pompeii and Herculaneum (and their inhabitants) were victims of these destructive events.

Tungurahua

Located in Ecuador's Cordillera Oriental mountain range, Tungurahua (meaning "Throat of Fire" in Quechua) is an active stratovolcano that has erupted with devastating force a number of times. It continues to pose a risk for inhabitants of local towns and villages

Katia Krafft

Because of the high temperatures and toxic gases produced by erupting volcanoes, the Kraffts wore special protective equipment when they ventured close to the lava flows. Designed for firefighters, fire proximity suits coated in reflective aluminum shielded them from the heat, and breathing apparatus provided them with safe air to breathe.

VOLCANO EXPLORERS

Katia Krafft and her husband Maurice were French volcanologists who made documentary movies about active volcanic eruptions. Both had been fascinated by volcanoes as children. When they met at college in the 1960s, they discovered their shared passion and, after they had finished their studies, they visited the volcanic island of Stromboli, where they documented the near-constant eruption of this Mediterranean volcano.

The photographs they took of Stromboli were popular with both experts and the public alike. Magazines and newspapers paid them for their images, which provided them with the funds to continue documenting eruptions all over the world. For the next 20 years, they traveled far and wide, flying directly to eruption sites, where they often climbed right up to the crater in search of active lava flows.

Their work would also have a great impact on public safety. In 1985, they made a film of the eruption of the Colombian volcano Nevado del Ruiz. This was a particularly dangerous and destructive event that triggered massive volcanic mudslides known as LAHARS. These occur when the hot lava melts the summit snowcap, adding vast amounts of water to the material flowing downhill. In this eruption, the lahars buried the nearby town of Armero, with a great loss of life. Many people around the world saw the devastation caused by this eruption, including the President of the Philippines—Maria Corazon Aquino. When a volcano—Mount Pinatubo—became active on the Filipino island of Luzon in 1991, the memory of the Krafft's film prompted Aquino to organize an evacuation of the area, with more than 60,000 people being moved to the capital Manilla. It proved to be a well-judged decision, because the eruption of Pinatubo was one of the largest in recent memory.

UNDERWATER VOLCANOES

As well as the volcanoes we can see on land or rising above the surface of the sea, there are many more submerged on the floors of the oceans. They are concentrated along the boundaries between ocean plates—these areas are known as OCEAN RIDGES. Underwater eruptions form the majority of volcanic activity on Earth. When these volcanoes break through the ocean surface, they form volcanic islands.

When seawater is drawn into volcanic fissures in these areas, it is heated to especially high temperatures by the hot magma within and escapes as bubbling gassy clouds known as HYDROTHERMAL VENTS.

In 1976, exploration along an ocean ridge near the Galapagos Islands revealed such activity. The following year, a team of scientists returned with DSV *Alvin*—a specialized submersible designed for undersea exploration at great depths. The team used *Alvin* to explore the Galapagos ridge, which revealed chimneylike rock structures releasing huge clouds of dark material. The team christened these BLACK SMOKERS. The dark color comes from sulfurous minerals that the hot water releases from the surrounding crust.

Hydrothermal vents are usually home to huge concentrations of life. Bacteria feed on minerals and nutrients released by the vents, and these in turn are consumed by plankton, which are then eaten by shrimp, worms, and fish. Certain species have become particularly well-adapted to the high temperatures surrounding the vents. These are known as EXTREMOPHILES.

WOODS HOLE OCEANOGRAPHIC INSTITUTE

ALVIN

DSV Alvin

Deep Submergence Vehicle (DSV) *Alvin* has been in service since 1964. It is about 23 feet long and weighs 22.5 tons. Its extremely strong titanium hull can withstand the immense pressures encountered at great depths. Such explorations often involve diving to its depth limit of about 14,800 feet during missions of 10 hours

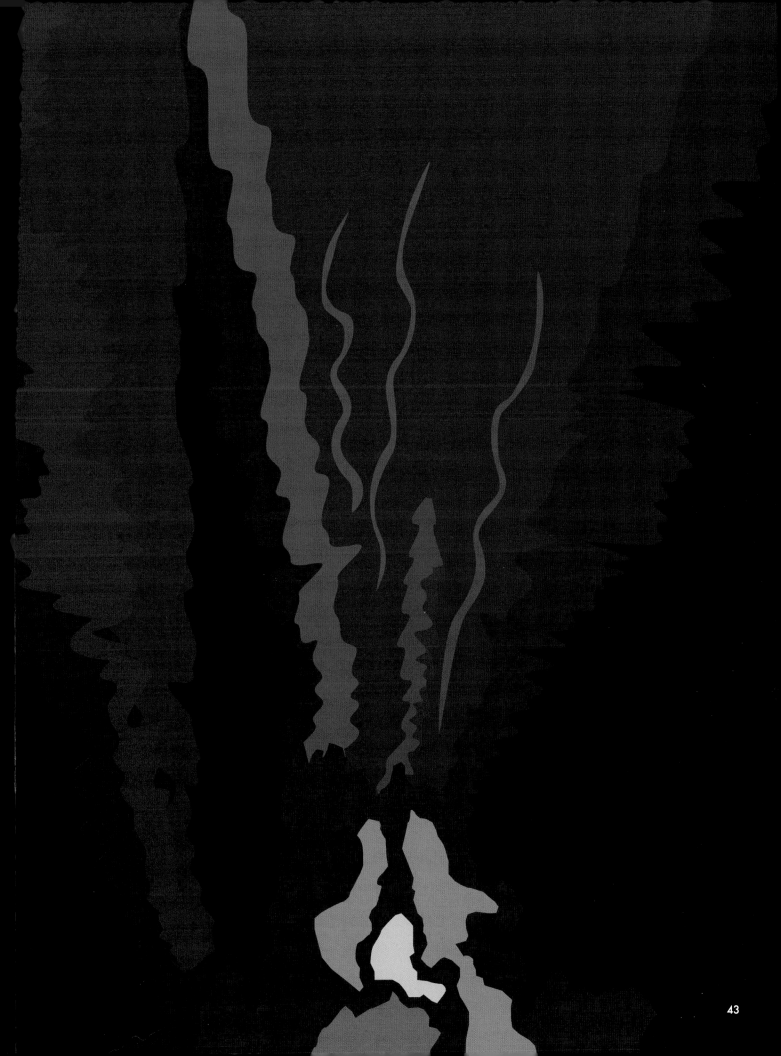

THE OCEANS

Immense bodies of water surrounding the continents, the oceans cover an amazing 71 percent of Earth's surface. They are home to a huge variety of wildlife, from tiny bacteria, algae, and plankton to large mammals ,such as whales, dolphins, and seals. The underwater environment is also the location of complex ecosystems, such as kelp forests, coral reefs, and seagrass meadows. In fact, the vast majority of life on our planet is hidden beneath the waves.

Ocean currents, waves, and tides shape our coastlines, and the oceans have a profound effect on Earth's atmosphere and climate, with photosynthetic phytoplankton producing the majority of the oxygen we breathe.

Humankind has explored the oceans for many thousands of years. Ever since the first primitive boats and rafts were constructed, the oceans have provided humans with food, a means of transport, and endless possibilities for exploration. Because of their vast scale, however, it took many years before we developed the most rudimentary picture of their shape and scale.

The earliest known ocean exploration took place around the coasts of the Mediterranean Sea. Later, both the Egyptians and Polynesian peoples of the Pacific Ocean developed sailing technology, which allowed for greater distances to be covered on the water. The latter explored far and wide across the Pacific, developing navigation techniques, mapping, and designs for canoes with outriggers to provide stability in rough seas.

The Scandinavian Norse people reached Iceland and Greenland, continued across the Atlantic Ocean about 1000 CE, and established settlements on today's Newfoundland and the Gulf of Saint Lawrence.

The golden age of ocean exploration came later, with famous European explorers, such as Christopher Columbus, Vasco de Gama, and Ferdinand Magellan, forging paths across the seas in search of distant lands.

The British Challenger expedition at the end of the nineteenth century was one of the first dedicated to the emerging science of OCEANOGRAPHY. Its mission was to study a great variety of marine phenomenon, from the chemical composition of seawater to the depth and temperature of the oceans, as well as to chart the diversity of plants and animals living in the seas or on the seafloor.

EARLY OCEAN EXPLORATION

The Polynesian peoples of the Pacific Ocean were the first great seafaring civilization. Originating from Taiwan and the surrounding mainland of southeast Asia, around 3000 years ago they began to explore the seas around today's Indonesia and the Philippines. As they traveled farther east, they practiced and refined their navigational techniques, using the stars, records of ocean currents and wave patterns, and even an understanding of the migratory patterns of birds.

Over a period of about 2000 years, Polynesian navigators explored a vast swathe of the Pacific Ocean, reaching as far as the islands of Hawaii in the north, Easter Island in the East, and New Zealand in the south.

Polynesian drua

Designed for long-distance exporation, the Polynesia drua is a large twin-hulled sailing boat. The hulls were made from planks of wood and could reach 100 feet long. Typically, they had a large covered shelter constructed in the center of the deck between the hulls. It provided refuge from bad weather as well as storage for food, firewood, hunting, and fishing equipment.

A tough, seafaring people from Scandinavia, the Vikings achieved amazing feats of long-distance ocean travel between the eighth and eleventh centuries CE. They developed vessels known as longships that were capable of crossing great distances in often adverse conditions, and they gained the navigational skills required to guide them while at sea.

The Vikings first explored the seas around Scandinavia and then pushed on farther afield. They traveled as far as the north of Africa and the south of Italy, both of which were reached via the Mediterranean. They ventured across the North Atlantic ocean, leaving settlements on today's Faroe Islands, Iceland, Greenland, and North America.

Viking longship

The Viking longship was strongly built but lightweight, with a shallow draft. This meant that it could operate in shallow waters and perform beach landings. It had a sail made of woven wool and oars to continue moving when there was not enough wind. The ship's relative lack of weight meant that it could be carried onto land and, with the mast removed, flipped over to form a temporary shelter.

Map labels:
BAFFIN ISLAND
GREENLAND
SHETLAND
CAPE ARAGO
DRAKES BAY
LISBON
CADIZ
CANARY ISLANDS
CUBA
HUATULCO
HAITI
CAPE VERDE ISLANDS
GUAYAQUIL
LIMA
ARICA
SANTA LUCIA BAY
VALPARAISO
RIO DE LA PLATA
STRAITS OF MAGELLAN
CAPE HORN

THE AGE OF EXPLORATION

The great maritime expeditions of the fifteenth and sixteenth centuries revealed a great deal about the geographical layout of the world's continents.

These expeditions were undoubtedly impressive, with great displays of bravery, skill, and conquest. Their lasting legacy was the beginnings of global maritime trading, which has shaped the modern world.

However, some were also responsible for tyrannical colonization, the emergence of the slave trade, and great acts of cruelty to indigenous peoples around the world.

Christopher Columbus

An Italian born in 1451, Christopher Columbus's first voyage departed the Spanish port of Palos de la Frontera on August 3, 1492. His crew were spread over three ships—the *Santa María*, the *Niña*, and the *Pinta*—which sailed to the Canary Islands and then across the Atlantic Ocean. On October 12, they sighted land—an island in the Bahamas. Their expedition took them onward to the north coast of Cuba. On Christmas Day 1492, the *Santa María* ran aground on the island of Haiti.

Columbus returned to Spain via the Azores. On this leg of the journey, he traveled on the *Niña*, which encountered terrible storms in the mid-Atlantic. Columbus went on to make three more great voyages of discovery.

Vasco de Gama

Born in the 1460s, Vasco de Gama was a Portuguese explorer whose first voyage sailed from Lisbon on July 8, 1497. Spread over four ships, led by his flagship the *São Gabriel*, they followed a course south around the continent of Africa, with stops at Tenerife and the Cape Verde islands. They sailed around the Cape of Good Hope, and continued up the east African coast, before setting out across the Indian Ocean. They reached the Malabar Coast in southern India, becoming the first Europeans to reach the country.

Many of de Gama's sailors died on the return journey and one of the ships was lost. The voyage was judged a success, and the spices they returned with helped to fund two more expeditions.

THE PHILIPPINES

THE SPICE ISLANDS

GOA

KOZHIKODI

MOMBASA

TIMOR

ST HELENA
BAY

CAPE OF GOOD HOPE

Ferdinand Magellan ——

Born in 1480, Ferdinand Magellan was a
Portuguese explorer who led an expedition to
discover a new route to the Maluku Islands,
known as the Spice Islands because of the
valuable nutmeg, mace, and cloves found
there. His fleet of five ships was led by
the *Trinidad*, and they departed Seville on
August 10,1519.

They crossed the Atlantic and traversed
a passage across to the Pacific Ocean—a
route now known as the Strait of Magellan.

Magellan himself was killed in a battle in the
Philippines. The voyage continued onward
to the Spice Islands, then Brunei and Timor
before crossing the Indian Ocean and home
via the Cape of Good Hope. It was the first
global circumnavigation in history.

Sir Francis Drake ——

Born around 1540, Sir Francis Drake was
an English explorer who was sent on a
voyage of discovery by Queen Elizabeth
I of England. He set out with five ships on
December 13, 1577.

The expedition took him and his crew to
North Africa, across the Atlantic, down the
east coast of South America, around the
treacherous Cape Horn, and then up the
west coast of the Americas as far as
modern-day California.

They then crossed the Pacific Ocean to the
Spice Islands, before continuing home via
Africa and Cape Verde.

Drake arrived back on 26th September 1580
with a single ship—the Golden Hind—after
all the others were lost. The voyage was the
second global circumnavigation.

Martin Frobisher ——

Born in the 1530s, Martin Frobisher
was an English explorer who led an
expedition in search of the Northwest
Passage—a possible trade route to Asia
via the northern reaches of the Americas.

Departing London on June 7, 1576, the
expedition sailed northward, stopping
at the Shetland Islands before crossing
the north Atlantic. They passed close by
Greenland, before landing at modern-day
Baffin Island.

Wind and cold forced him and his crew
to return home. They made two more
expeditions, landing on Greenland and
exploring farther westward, but failed to
find the Northwest Passage.

49

VESSELS OF EXPLORATION

The marine expeditions that took place during the great age of exploration required sturdy, well-built ships capable of sustaining good speed across the uncharted oceans of the world. Such ships employed multiple sails to ensure progress could be made, even in light winds. Their large, heavy hulls remained balanced in rough, stormy seas, and they proved to be reliable during the many months they spent exploring distant regions of the world.

Santa María

Christopher Columbus's flagship the *Santa María* was built in Pontevedra in the Spanish region of Galicia, and it first launched in 1460. She was a CARRACK—a three-masted sailing ship designed to be stable in rough seas, with storage space for the many provisions required for long-distance voyages, as well as room for cargo on the return journey.

After it ran aground off the island of Haiti, the crew dismantled the ship and used the wood to build a fort. Columbus named the fort La Navidad ("Christmas" in Spanish), because the *Santa María* had run aground on Christmas Day.

Victoria

Victoria was the only ship to survive Ferdinand Magellan's global circumnavigation. Also a carrack, it was built in Gipuzkoa, in the Basque region of Spain, and first launched in 1519.

When the *Victoria* returned home to Spain, it was in poor condition. Its sails were ripped and shredded, and the hull was damaged and leaking— the crew were continually bailing it out. She was repaired, however, and continued sailing as a merchant vessel until it was lost in the Atlantic Ocean in 1570.

Golden Hind

When Sir Francis Drake set off on his circumnavigation, his flagship was known as the *Pelican*, which had first been launched in 1577. However, during the voyage he renamed it the *Golden Hind*, after the crest of his sponsor, Sir Christopher Hatton. It was a GALLEON —an evolution of the carrack that was longer and lower, and with a more complex (but efficient) sail layout. It was crewed by 80 men.

After Drake's voyage, the *Golden Hind* joined the English Armada during the Anglo-Spanish War. Drake led this military expedition against the Spanish but it was unsuccessful, and many ships and men were lost.

THE CHALLENGER EXPEDITION

In 1872, a British expedition set sail from Portsmouth, England, on an unprecedented voyage of scientific exploration. HMS *Challenger* was a steam-assisted sailing ship, commanded by Captain George Nares. The scientific team was led by Charles Wyville Thomson of the University of Edinburgh. The aim of the expedition was to study the nature of the world's oceans—the oceans themselves as awell as the plants and animals living within them.

The Challenger expedition forged a circuitous route around the world. During a journey lasting four years and covering a distance of 79,275 miles, the ship explored the North and South Atlantic before heading east via South Africa and the coast of Antarctica to Australia. It then went around Indonesia and the Philippines, on to Japan, and across the Pacific Ocean via Hawaii to Chile. Finally, it went south, around Tierra del Fuego, before heading back to England.

During the voyage, detailed measurements were taken of the ocean's depths and temperatures, weather conditions, and samples were taken from the seabed. Marine specimens were collected with nets and dredges, which were then sorted and preserved for the journey home.

At one sampling stop in the south Pacific, they encountered a particularly deep area of seabed. Their measurments recorded a depth of 26,850 feet—this spot is now known to be part of the Mariana Trench—the deepest area on the surface of Earth. Their sampling point is now named after the vessel—Challenger Deep—and modern measurements nearby have shown the deepest point to be an amazing 36,070 feet.

As the first expedition dedicated to the study of the oceans, Challenger was a groundbreaking endeavor that provided huge insight into the nature and history of the marine world.

HMS *Challenger*

Designed as a small warship, HMS *Challenger* was a three-masted wooden sailing ship, with additional power provided by a powerful steam engine. For the expedition, 15 of its guns were removed to make more room for the scientific equipment and laboratories on board. It was about 225 feet long, and carried more than 200 crew, officers, and scientists. The United States space shuttle *Challenger* was named after the ship.

MODERN OCEANOGRAPHY

Today, the science of oceanography is carried out by the crew of specialized research vessels, such as the American ship *Ronald H. Brown*, which is operated by the U.S. National Oceanic and Atmospheric Administration (NOAA).

Such ships are designed to conduct research at sea for prolonged periods all around the world. They usually feature a rugged construction. The *Ronald H. Brown* has a hardened steel hull, which allows for it to use its powerful engines to break through sea ice in the polar regions. The ship carries winches, cranes, and other lifting devices, which let it lower and haul heavy cables and scientific devices for measuring and taking samples deep below the surface of the sea.

Above the water, modern research vessels carry instruments for studying the atmosphere and weather, such as high-accuracy radar equipment that can provide imagery of ocean storm systems.

Below deck, laboratories and computer systems provide the ship's scientists with everything they need to develop data from their ocean and atmospheric measurements and analyze samples taken from the sea and ocean floor.

The *Ronald H. Brown* has traveled more than 150,000 miles, during which time it has surveyed the floor of the American continental shelf, investigated the ecology of the coast of Alaska, mapped remote reefs in the Pacific Ocean, and undertaken many other valuable scientific missions.

NOASS *Ronald H. Brown*

The *Ronald H. Brown* is 275 feet long and is powered by diesel engines and electrical generators. It carries a crew of 26 and up to 30 scientists on board. It is the largest ship in the NOAA fleet and, when it is not out at sea on operations, it is based at the port of Charleston, South Carolina.

UNDERSEA EXPLORATION

Exploring the depths of the oceans has fascinated humankind for hundreds of years. In ancient Greece, divers would use rocks to help them descend to the seafloor to collect sponges, shells, and coral. Japanese divers, known as AMA, dived down to extract valuable pearls from oysters. Throughout Japanese history, ama have mostly been women.

In the sixteenth and seventeenth centuries, nautical engineers constructed the first DIVING BELLS and diving suits. Both let people breathe underwater: the first by trapping air inside a metal tank and the second by supplying air to a sealed suit with a hose running to the surface. These were used both for scientific endeavors and to salvage valuable equipment from the wrecks of sunken ships.

In 1925, the French naval officer Yves Le Prieur invented SCUBA equipment. Scuba stands for self-contained underwater breathing apparatus. Le Prieur's equipment consisted of a tank that supplied compressed air to a breathing mouthpiece via a regulator, which reduced the flow of air so it was easy to breathe. This design was later updated by the well-known underwater adventurer Jacques Cousteau, who named the new device the Aqua-Lung.

Scuba diving gave scientists and explorers the freedom to spend prolonged periods underwater, greatly increasing their understanding of the flora and fauna both in the water and on the seafloor. It was dangerous, however, especially when divers tried to descend deeper. If equipment failed at depth, returning safely to the surface could be difficult. Decompression sickness, known as THE BENDS, could occur if a diver ascended through the water too quickly.

Various techniques were later developed to allow for divers to dive deeper safely and for longer. These included special mixtures of gases (instead normal air), "rebreather" equipment (which recycled the gases instead of releasing them into the water with each exhalation), and pressurized suits. The latter are rigid metal apparatus that allow dives as deep as 2,300 feet with virtually none of the dangers of conventional diving.

Dr. Sylvia Earle (left) is a renowned marine biologist and underwater explorer. In the early 1970s, she led a team living aboard the long-term underwater laboratory Tektite, in the U.S. Virgin Islands. In 1979, she used a pressurised JIM suit to set a new female deep dive record when she dived to a depth of 1,250 feet off the coast of the Hawaiian island of Oahu. As well as her scientific and environmental work, she has been involved in the development of both manned and unmanned deep-sea exploration equipment.

THE DESERTS

Scattered across the surface of Earth are areas in which little water falls as rain. The effects of the sun and wind cause soil and rocks to break down. This process is called DENUDATION, and the remaining landscapes are classed as deserts. Some deserts, such as the vast Sahara, are sandy; others, such as the Mojave in California, are made up of compacted pebbles worn by the wind known as a DESERT PAVEMENT. Some are covered by a white crust that is left when annual meltwater from nearby mountains evaporates in the summer sun, leaving behind salt deposits. Despite the thick ice covering its surface, much of Antarctica is classed as desert, because of the low amount of water (in the form of snow) that falls every year.

Deserts pose tremendous challenges to plants, animals, and humans living within their borders. The environment is harsh, and water and shelter are scarce. Many species have evolved characteristics that enable them to survive and even flourish in these conditions.

Humans have lived and traveled across deserts for thousands of years. The indigenous peoples of southern Africa and Australia both developed sophisticated skills that have helped them to find water, track animals, and forage for edible plants in the desert lands through which they traveled. Later, traders often traveled across deserts, such as the Tuareg peoples of the Sahara. They transported goods such as salt, textiles, gold, and saffron, in camel convoys known as caravans.

Desert exploration became popular in the nineteenth century, with a variety of impressive journeys undertaken around the world. Initially, camels were the favored form of transportation but, with the invention of the car in the early twentieth century, some explorers, such Sweden's Eva Dickson, have used this new technology to tackle longer and more challenging routes.

THE SAHARA

Stretching across the northern countries of the continent of Africa, the Sahara is the largest hot desert on Earth. It covers an area of about 2.5 million square miles, around the same size as the United States or China. The Sahara is home to an Algerian village— Bou Bernous—that boasts the highest average high temperature in the world: 116.6 degrees Fahrenheit.

Geographically, it is a mixture of flat, stony plateaus (known as *hamada* in Arabic), and rolling seas of windswept sand dunes (known as *ergs* in Arabic). Some areas of the Sahara are more mountainous, with volcanic peaks rising from the desert floor across its southern reaches.

The extreme arid climate of the Sahara presents a great challenge to plant and animal life. The flora is largely made up of grasses, palm trees, and spiky shrubs, adapted to the hot, drying wind. As well as snakes, lizards, and scorpions, animal life includes the fennec fox, which has evolved large ears to help radiate its body heat.

Saharan trade routes

Traders have explored and crossed the Sahara since prehistoric times. Over the past 2,000 years, trade routes became established that let caravans of camels transport goods of various kinds from countries on the southern side of the Sahara northeast to Egypt and the Middle East, and also to ports on the north side of the desert for onward shipment to Europe.

The routes outlined in the map above were the main paths taken by caravans of traders in the fifteenth century. Although camels have largely been replaced with trucks and freight trains, there are still traders using camels to transport salt on the southern fringes of the Sahara.

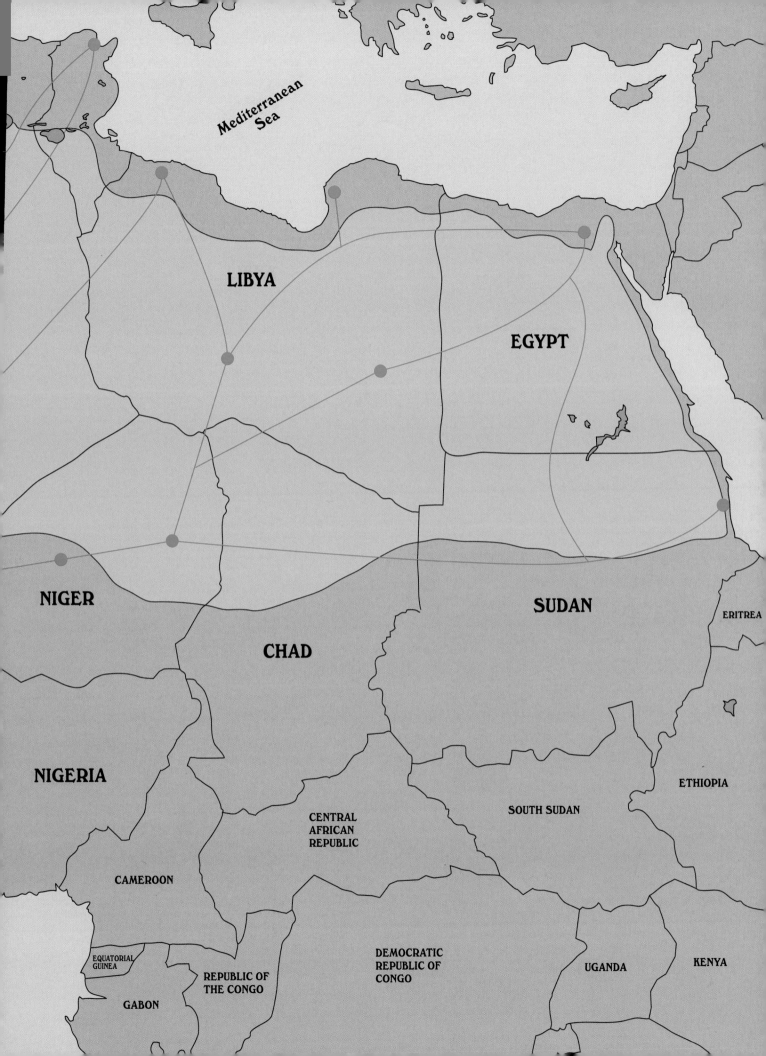

THE EMPTY QUARTER

The Rub' al Khali (Arabic for the "Empty Quarter") is the largest area of continuous sandy desert in the world. It is the central part of the Arabian Desert, which stretches from Jordan in the north to Oman in the south. Temperatures here soar to above 122 degrees Fahrenheit in the summer.

The first European to cross the Empty Quarter was the explorer Bertram Thomas, who completed the journey in 1929. In the 1940s, British adventurer Wilfred Thesiger made a number of journeys around and across the Empty Quarter, learning about the Bedouin people and how they lived in this desolate place.

Thesiger was born in Ethiopia, and he returned to Africa after attending university in England. He explored Darfur and the Upper Nile, remote regions that are both part of modern Sudan. During World War II, he served with the newly formed Special Operations Executive and Special Air Service in both the Middle East and North Africa.

Following the war, he was hired by an antilocust unit operated by the United Nations. They wanted to know about locust breeding grounds within the Empty Quarter, which gave the curious Thesiger a reason to explore the region.

Thesiger had studied the reports Thomas had made about his crossing, and realized that, in order to travel safely, he would have to learn the desert skills and customs from the native Bedouin people.

Thesiger made two crossings of the Empty Quarter, both accompanied by Bedouin tribesmen. He recorded the journeys, taking plenty of photographs and making detailed maps of the region that showed the locations of important features, such as oases (where they could collect water) and treacherous areas of quicksand.

The journeys were dangerous not only due to the perils of the desert itself but also because of tribal and political tension in the area. Local desert rulers treated foreigners with suspicion, and some of Thesiger's guides refused to travel with him after confrontations with other tribesmen. Later, he and his guides were imprisoned by the king of Saudi Arabia.

The Empty Quarter itself remains just as desolate and unforgiving as it was in Thesiger's day.

Arabian camel
Camelus dromedarius

Also known as the dromedary, the Arabian camel is a large mammal well-adapted to life in the arid heat of the desert. Grazing on tough, thorny plants and dry grasses, it is able to build up fat reserves in the hump on its back. During periods when food and water are scarce, it can use the reserves in its hump to sustain itself until it can eat and drink again.

Great Victoria Desert

Stretching over an area of 135,000 square miles, the Great Victoria Desert is the largest in Australia. Straddling the states of Western Australia and South Australia, it is home to Australian Aboriginal communities, including those of the Mirning and Pitjantjatjara peoples.

The first European to cross the desert was the explorer Ernest Giles. Having emigrated to Australia from England in the 1850s, Giles went on to lead a number of daring expeditions across the outback. He crossed the Great Victoria Desert in 1875, departing South Australia's Port Augusta on May 23 with a caravan of camels. Having been unable to find water in the central part of the desert, the expedition was saved when an Aboriginal man led them to a hidden spring. They pushed on, reaching Perth on the western coast on November 18.

Spinifex
Triodia basedowii

A dense grass species that forms lumpy hummocks on the desert floor, spinifex is found throughout the arid outback of Australia. Its dense, sharply pointed leaves have been used traditionally by Australian Aboriginal people for making hunting implements, and the sticky resin within for fixing spearheads.

Mojave Desert

Home to the fearsome-sounding Furnace Creek and Death Valley, the Mojave is the driest desert in North America. Located across the southern stretches of the states of California and Nevada, it is bordered by the San Gabriel Mountains and San Bernadino Mountains to the south and the Tehachapi Mountains to the west.

The Mojave is home to a variety of specially-adapted plant and animal life. The Joshua tree is its most famous resident, a spiky-leaved member of the yucca family that can reach heights of 50 feet. Animal species include the venomous Western diamondback rattlesnake, tarantula spiders, and large predators, such as coyotes and cougars.

ACROSS THE GOBI

In 2018, the Polish adventurer Mateusz Waligóra set off alone, on foot, on a journey across a section of the Gobi Desert. The Gobi is a barren rocky desert bordered by the Himalayas and the Altai mountains and stretches across a broad swathe of northern China and southern Mongolia. Because of the complications of traveling in that part of China, Waligóra decided to concentrate solely on the Mongolian portion of the desert.

To carry his equipment and supplies, Waligóra designed and constructed a trailer that he would tow via a harness attached around his waist. This would let him transport plenty of water—sometimes up to 25 gallons at a time which, along with clothing, food, a tent, and other essentials (not to mention the cart itself) weighed more than 440 pounds in total. Part of the reason for this is because Waligóra wanted to make his crossing unassisted, unlike previous expeditions that had relied on camels, food drops, and rendezvous points along the way.

The conditions were challenging—he encountered numerous sandstorms and had to endure a wide range of temperatures, from baking sunshine during the day to freezing cold during the night. The wheels of his trailer were damaged as a result of the rough ground—many of the spokes broke—and he found himself regularly patching punctures.

However, the journey was successful. After 58 days, Mateusz Waligóra became the first person to cross the Mongolian Gobi alone on foot and, in doing so, he covered an amazing 1,110 miles.

RIVERS

Long, flowing bodies of water that crisscross the continents, rivers can take many forms, from raging, mountain torrents to slow-moving watercourses spreading out toward the sea.

Rivers flow from a point or area known as the source. River sources can be icy water from melting snow or glaciers, rainwater draining down mountains, or from wet, marshy land. They can also take the form of springs, releasing water from underground sources known as AQUIFERS. Rivers then follow a path known as a COURSE until they flow into a larger body of water at the MOUTH. A river mouth can occur when a smaller river meets a larger one, when it reaches a lake, or upon meeting a sea or ocean. The area of land through which the river (and any smaller rivers that flow into it known as TRIBUTARIES) flows is known as the RIVER BASIN.

The energy carried by the river's moving water can have profound effects on the shape of the land through which it flows. Over time, rivers can carve deep valleys through hilly terrain. Sometimes these take the form of canyons with steep sides, which occur when river courses flow over high plateaus. As the water exposes and wears down the ground material that least resists its action, this material is eroded. This process causes the tougher rocky surrounding ground to remain as sheer cliffs on each side of the river, which drops deeper and deeper between them.

Humankind has lived in close proximity to rivers throughout history. There are many reasons for this. They provide fresh drinking water, can be used to irrigate crops, and are home to fish and other aquatic life that provide food. They are also used for transportation and can drive energy systems, such as watermills.

Rivers have long fascinated explorers. As natural transportation routes, curious travelers would often follow rivers upstream in search of the source. Because rivers provide access into landscapes that are difficult to access via other methods (such as the dense rain forest surrounding the Amazon River in South America), they gave early naturalists a means of discovering these places. In the nineteenth century scientists, such as Alexander von Humbolt and Alfred Russel Wallace, conducted lengthy fieldwork expeditions in the Amazon River basin.

Tiger Leaping Gorge

The spectacular canyon known as the Tiger Leaping Gorge is part of the Jinsha River, a tributary of the Upper Yangtze River in Yunnan province, China.

The gorge is one of the deepest canyons in the world, with a drop of 12,434 feet from the adjoining mountain peak to river level.

Yukon

Mackenzie

Missouri

Mississippi

Rio
Grande

Niger

RIVERS AROUND THE WORLD

Orinoco

Amazon

Parana

The world's great rivers stretch across the continents, carving huge gorges and valleys on the way to their mouths.

Many originate in the high mountains, where melting snow and ice create the streams that join to form rivers, such as the Ganges, the Indus, and the Mekong.

Others, such as the Zambezi, originate in marshy wetland areas, where streams flow from the waterlogged ground.

The Nile is the longest river in the world, flowing across 11 African countries during its 4,130-mile journey from its source in the mountains of Burundi to its extensive delta on the Egyptian coast, where it flows into the Mediterranean Sea.

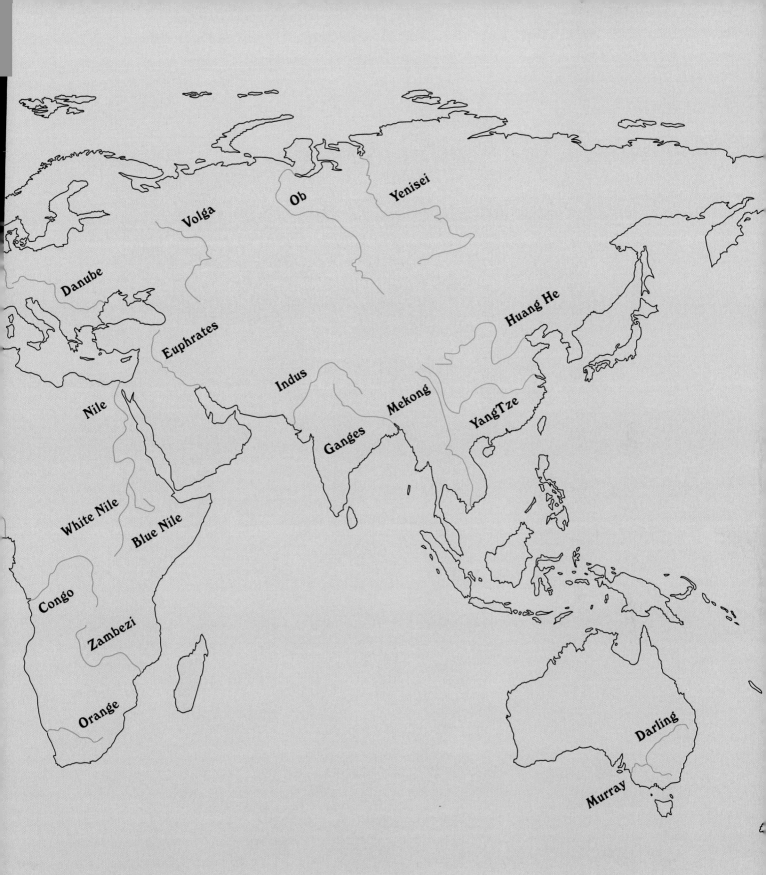

EXPLORING THE WHITE NILE

Sir Samuel Baker and his wife Florence were British explorers who set out in March 1861 to explore central Africa and to search for the source of the Nile. Initially, they focused on the area around the borders of modern-day Ethiopia and Sudan. Various tributaries of the Nile flow through this area, such as the Tekezé, which runs from the Ethiopian Highlands before joining the Atbarah River (sometimes known as the Black Nile), which then joins the Nile itself.

They then traveled from the Sudanese city of Khartoum along the White Nile toward its source. During this leg of their journey, they met John Hanning Speke and Richard Francis Burton, another pair of British explorers who had been the first Europeans to discover Lake Victoria during their own search for the source of the Nile. They were convinced that this lake was the main source of the river, but while much water did flow from this point, they were unaware of the more distant Kagera River, which fed into Lake Victoria from its origins in the Burundian uplands.

Samuel and Florence traveled onward into modern-day Uganda, where they became the first Europeans to discover a lake that they named Lake Albert, after Queen Victoria's late consort. Speke and Burton had previously named Lake Victoria after the Queen.

Samuel Baker became convinced that this newly discovered lake was a major source of the Nile, although later research showed that it provided only a fraction of the flow from Lake Victoria and beyond.

Samuel and Florence followed the White Nile beyond Lake Albert and, in doing so, discovered an impressive waterfall. The river flowed through a narrow, rocky gorge, and then dropped 138 feet to the pool below before flowing onward. They named it Murchison Falls, after the president of the Royal Geographical Society.

They returned to Khartoum in 1865 and traveled back to England the following year. Samuel Baker published accounts of their travels in Africa, and he was awarded the gold medal of the Royal Geographical Society in recognition of the discoveries.

THE AMAZON ON FOOT

In April 2008, the British explorer Ed Stafford began a grueling and ambitious attempt to walk the length of the Amazon River from source to sea. Over the following 859 days and 4,500 miles, he followed the river, occasionally using an inflatable raft to carry his equipment. However, whenever he had to cross the river, he made sure to start walking again at a point perpendicular to where he crossed from. This way, he knew that the entire journey would have been made without having used the flow of the river to make forward progress.

He started the expedition with a British companion, but the two struggled to get along, so Ed continued alone until he was joined by a Peruvian—Gadiel "Cho" Sanchez Rivera. The pair stayed together all the way until the end, where the Amazon meets the Atlantic Ocean.

The expedition presented them with all kinds of challenges and perilous encounters on an almost daily basis. They struggled to carry enough food to offset the enormous physical efforts they put in every day, so occasionally they had to resort to foraging for wild bananas and nuts as well as hunting piranha fish and tortoises.

They regularly encountered venomous snakes, and they were stung by scorpions and bitten by ants and mosquitoes. They also had confrontations with Colombian criminal gangs and armed tribesmen, who took them prisoner until they were able to apologize to the chief for crossing the perimeters of the tribe's land.

The expedition marked the first time that the Amazon had been followed along its entirety on foot, and the journey was also later recognized as the longest jungle trek in history.

THE MACKENZIE RIVER EXPEDITION

The Scottish explorer Sir Alexander Mackenzie made a number of impressive expeditions across the North American continent in the late eighteenth century. Having moved to the United States as a boy, he then settled in Montreal, Canada, during the American Revolutionary War. At the age of 24, he helped to establish a fur trading post called Fort Chipewayan on the shores of Lake Athabasca.

From here, he set out, in 1789, on a canoe expedition up the river, which was flowing from the lake in a northwesterly direction. It flowed into another body of water, Great Slave Lake, and then onward north. Mackenzie hoped that the river would eventually flow out into the Pacific Ocean, providing passage across the continent from east to west. However, he was dismayed to find that it flowed out into the Arctic Ocean on Canada's north coast.

The section of the river from Great Slave Lake to the Arctic Ocean was renamed after Mackenzie some years later. It was previously known by the name given by the indigenous Canadians as Dehcho (meaning "big river").

Undaunted, Mackenzie set out again in 1792. This time he traveled up one of the rivers that flowed into Lake Athabasca, the Peace River. He and his team followed it westward, which led them into the mountains of the Great Divide. They hauled their birch bark canoes through the Coast Mountains and discovered a route via the Bella Coola River that took them to the Pacific Ocean. It was not a practical trade route, because of the mountain crossing, but Mackenzie's expedition marked the first crossing of the North American continent from east to west.

JUNGLES AND FORESTS

Jungles and forests are areas of Earth in which trees and other plants dominate the environment. There is an incredible diversity of such areas, from the dense tropical rain forests of South America, Africa, and Southeast Asia to northern snow forests, known as TAIGA, which dominate Alaska, Canada, Scandinavia, and northern Russia.

Ecologically, these areas are incredibly important. Trees and other large vegetation convert carbon dioxide in the atmosphere into new plant material, capturing it until they themselves breakdown and are ingested or absorbed by other plants or animals. This process produces oxygen, which we need to breathe. Tree cover also protects the soil beneath from erosion by rain and wind.

Many types of smaller plants and fungi live in and around the trees, which provide protection within the TREE CANOPY—the area between the ground and the tops of trees. The tree canopy can have one or more layers in which the temperature, sunlight, and amount of moisture varies. These are known as MICROCLIMATES. The bigger the tree canopy, the more potential microclimates it can accommodate, and the greater number of species it can provide a home for.

Humankind has lived within forests for thousands of years. The trees provide shelter and building materials, and the plant life and animals within them provide food.

Greater bird-of-paradise
Paradisaea apoda

The greater bird-of-paradise is found across the forests of New Guinea and the Indonesian Aru Islands. The male (shown here) has brightly colored plumage, which it uses to attract the attention of females during extensive courtship dances that are performed high in the tree canopy.

Wallace's flying frog
Rhacophorus nigropalmatus

Discovered by Alfred Russel Wallace and named after him, Wallace's flying frog is found in western Indonesia, Sumatra, and Borneo. Its fingers and toes are webbed, which lets it jump (descending gently) from within the tree canopy (where it spends most of its time) down to the forest floor. It has soft, sticky pads on its toes and fingers, which cushion landings and also help it stick to branches and tree trunks while climbing.

JUNGLE EVOLUTION

Alfred Russel Wallace was a British naturalist and explorer who led some of the most ambitious zoological expeditions ever undertaken. In doing so, he traveled through previously unexplored forests, discovering a host of new species in the process. Wallace also concluded that plants and animals evolve through the process of natural selection. Wallace's work strongly influenced Charles Darwin, who went on to become much better-known than Wallace when he published his own account of the nature of evolution—*On the Origin of Species*.

Wallace first traveled to the forests of Brazil with his colleague Henry Bates. Wallace's main aim was to investigate plant and animal species, particularly insects, in the Amazon rain forest. He focused on the area around the Rio Negro, a large tributary of the Amazon River. He spent four years in the forest, making notes and collecting and preserving specimens. Many of these he sent back home but, alas, when he finally traveled back to Great Britain, his ship *Helen* caught fire in the Atlantic Ocean and all the specimens on board were lost at sea. Wallace and the crew of the *Helen* spent days in an open lifeboat before they were rescued. Back home, he wrote papers and books about his travels in the Amazonian forests.

In 1854, Wallace set out again, this time to the Malay Archipelago—the island group now made up of Indonesia, Malaysia, and Singapore. He spent eight years there, observing, drawing, and noting down the behavior and nature of the species he found. He collected a huge number of specimens—125,660 in total, including 83,200 beetles and 13,100 butterflies and moths—and the study and classification of these strongly influenced his thinking about the possibility of plant and animal species evolving in response to the forces of natural selection.

He wrote a book about this expedition called *The Malay Archipelago*, in which he outlined the various locations he explored, their geography, and the people he found living there. It also described many of the species he had discovered, such as the various birds-of-paradise and the Wallace's flying frog (*Rhacophorus nigropalmatus*).

PROTECTING
FOREST ECOSYSTEMS

Because of the effects of human activities, such as logging and the clearing of woodland areas for agriculture and construction, many of the world's great forest areas are under threat. As forests are lost, so too are many of the plant and animal species that rely on them for shelter and food. The destruction of woodland areas is known as DEFORESTATION.

Trees provide stability for the underlying soil and prevent erosion. Their roots hold the soil together, and the leaves that drop from their canopies form litter, which protects the surface of the soil. The tree canopy also protects the soil from flash floods during heavy rainfall. When trees are cut down, the soil loses all of this protection. During rainstorms, it can break up and be washed away, sometimes causing landslides. Unprotected by leaf litter during hot summers, the remaining soil dries out and can become dusty and lifeless.

The world's forests, especially tropical rain forests, are home to the greatest concentrations of biodiversity on the planet. The effects of deforestation have profound effects on the animal and plant species that live within the woodland habitat. These species have evolved complex relationships with their environment and the other organisms that they share it with. When this environment is damaged or destroyed completely, the interconnected community of organisms dependent upon it undergoes a traumatic upheaval that, especially in the case of tropical rain forests, leads to many species becoming extinct. Surviving species typically undergo a significant drop in numbers, including microbes living within the soil.

In the 1970s, the United Nations set up a program with the aim of protecting precious and irreplaceable ecosystems around the world. These ecosystems are designated as World Biosphere Reserves. Within these areas, action is taken to conserve natural habitats and landscape features, such as rivers and lakes, as well as to preserve species numbers and diversity. In the areas around these protected reserves, educational projects aim to help the local population live and work in close proximity to the diverse ecosystem in a way that is environmentally sustainable.

This program has been incredibly successful, with nearly 700 biosphere reserves now existing in 122 countries around the world. These include tropical and forest areas, coastal, marine, and island sites, and mountain and desert areas.

Jiuzhaigou World Biosphere Reserve

Situated within the Minshan mountain range in the Chinese province of Sichuan, Jiuzhaigou is a UNESCO designated biosphere reserve. The area was previously heavily logged, until the Chinese government banned the activity and made it a national park. Since then it has recovered, and the magnificent forests of broad-leaved trees, rhododendron, and bamboo are home to species that include the rare golden snub-nosed monkey and the giant panda.

CAVES AND CHASMS

Hidden from view beneath the surface of Earth are spaces in the rocky crust. These are known as caves, and they are formed by a process called SPELEOGENESIS. Some are formed by the shifting of the crust's tectonic plates. Others, known as LAVA CAVES, are formed when erupting volcanoes release molten lava. Some of it can cool to form pipelike structures, through which the remaining lava can continue to flow. When the flow ceases, tubular lava caves remain. Glacier (or ice) caves form in the base of glaciers, where flowing water carves tunnels between the ice and the rock below.

The majority of caves are formed by water. As water from rain or rivers soaks down through the earth, it mixes with carbon dioxide in the soil and becomes acidic. Certain types of rock, such as limestone, can be dissolved by this acidic water in a process known as DISSOLUTION. The water eats through the rock, dissolving it and flowing deeper into the ground. If this mixture of water and limestone minerals flows over a surface or drips from a ceiling, it can form back into rock. Such formations can include sheets of rock known as FLOWSTONE, or long candlelike structures—STALACTITIES if they hang from a ceiling or STALAGMITES when they rise from the floor.

Throughout human history, caves have been used for shelter from the elements and from predators. Early humans decorated the walls of such caves with art, and also used certain areas as burial tombs.

Many species of plants and animals also make caves their home. Animal species that are adapted to live in caves and spend their entire lives within cave systems are known as TROGLOBITES. Because caves are permanently dark, these organisms typically have diminished eyesight or have become entirely blind. Instead, they have evolved other senses, with sensory antennae or enhanced smelling abilities to help them navigate their habitat. The scientific study of caves is known as SPELEOLOGY.

The exploration of caves became popular in the late nineteenth century and remains a popular activity. Many advances have been made, with modern equipment helping cavers to descend deep underground and to pass through water-filled sections in the branch of caving known as CAVE DIVING. Because of the unpredictability of the cave structure and possible flooding, caving remains a dangerous sport.

Cave of Swallows

Situated in central Mexico, the Cave of Swallows (*Sótano de las Golondrinas* in Spanish) is a huge open cave shaft—the largest known in the world. It drops nearly 1,300 feet from top to bottom. The walls of the cave are home to thousands of birds, from which the cave gets its name.

EARLY UNDERGROUND ADVENTURES

The first explorer to develop the activity we know today as caving was a Frenchman, Édouard-Alfred Martel, at the end of the nineteenth century. As a child, he was fascinated by the stories of Jules Verne, including *Journey to the Center of the Earth*. While on vacation with his parents in the Pyrenees, he first ventured into a cave system, and over the following years he made more trips to visit caves across Europe.

As Martel's caving expeditions became more adventurous, the equipment he required became more complex. He developed rope systems that let him descend safely to great depths. He carried ladders (including compact folding ones constructed from steel wire), which he left in place, letting him climb back up over smooth or slippery rocky sections. Certain cave systems he explored, such as the Caves of Drach on the Spanish island of Mallorca, featured underground lakes. To explore these, Martel lowered a wooden boat down through the entrance tunnels, which then let him navigate the waters below and measure the extent of these subterranean lakes.

Martel was also the first person to descend to the bottom of Gaping Gill, a deep open shaft in North Yorkshire, England. Previously a British explorer, John Birkbeck, had attempted this descent in 1842, but he had managed to drop only part of the way down. Martel descended the full 322 feet using ropes and ladders. Gaping Gill was thought to be the deepest-known cave shaft in Great Britain until the discovery of the Titan cavern in Derbyshire in 1999.

Over the course of his lifetime, Mantel explored more than 1,500 caves. In doing so, he pushed the boundaries of the sport of caving, and also helped establish the science of speleology. His investigations, measurements, and mapping of the underground world paved the way for many future scientists and adventurers.

Caves of Drach

The Spanish island of Mallorca is home to an underground system known as the Caves of Drach (*Cuevas del Drach*). These caverns were created by the dissolution effects of seawater from the Mediterranean flowing into cracks and fissures in the limestone rock that the island is formed from. The main area of water in the system is known as the Martel Lake,and is more than 330 feet in length.

THE DEEPEST CAVE ON EARTH

Located within the western Caucasus Mountains in Georgia, Veryovkina Cave is the deepest known in the world. It is named after the Russian cave explorer Alexander Veryovkin.

The cave has a relatively small entrance hole, around 10 feet in diameter. It leads into a shaft that drops 105 feet. This initial section was discovered by cave explorers in 1968. They continued downward via tunnels and reached a point 377 feet below the surface. Returning to the top, they marked the cave on their map and left.

It wasn't until the 1980s, when a caving team from Moscow arrived in the region, that Veryovkina was explored farther. Over the next few years, they discovered more tunnels that led them to a depth of 1,444 feet.

Members of the same team returned in 2000 and every year that followed. After 15 years, they discovered a new shaft that led them deeper underground. The system was massive and mapping its depths was complex and time-consuming. By 2018, they had reached a point 7,257 feet below the surface— Veryovkina became the deepest cave ever explored.

Living underground

The 2018 expedition to the base of Veryovkina Cave was led by the speleologists Pavel Demidov and Ilya Turbanov. It took their team of intrepid Russian explorers 12 days to descend and then reascend, eating and sleeping at preplanned camps during their journey. During the expedition, they discovered a variety of rare species living within the cave system.

CAVE DIVING

Many cave systems are filled with water or feature partly water-filled tunnels known as siphons. To pass through such terrain requires the use of scuba gear, and the activity is known as CAVE DIVING. Cave diving is a very specialized, complex, and potentially dangerous activity for a number of reasons. Unlike diving in the open sea, where the exit point (the surface) is obviously straight up, it involves penetrating water-filled systems, with route finding required to return to the start point.

Because of the possibility of narrow sections, scuba equipment is usually carried in a special arrangement, with gas tanks on the divers' side instead of on their back. It can also be demounted and pushed through particularly small sections. Brightly colored ropes called GUIDELINES are carried and unwound as divers swim deeper into the system. These can then be followed back out again—getting lost while cave diving is one of the greatest dangers. Rebreathing equipment is often used to give divers the maximum amount of time to explore while still providing enough supply in case of emergencies on the way back through the cave.

Dos Ojos

Meaning "two eyes" in Spanish, the Dos Ojos cave system is located in Mexico near the Caribbean coast of the Yucatan Peninsula. It is accessed via water-filled shafts known as CENOTES. The water is fresh near the surface, but mixes with salt water from the ocean in the deeper sections. Dos Ojos connects to the Sac Actun cave system, and together they form the longest-known underwater cave system in the world, stretching an amazing 215 miles along the Yucatan coast.

CAVES OF ICE

As the ice within glaciers melts, the water trickles down underneath, eventually forming streams that flow away down the sides of the mountain. The ice melts on the surface of the glacier and can carve tubular shaft structures known as MOULINS. Depending on the temperature of the meltwater, the flow through the moulins can cause spaces to form underneath the glacier, which are then enlarged over time with this repeated melting action. Such spaces are known as GLACIER CAVES. When glaciers occur in areas of volcanic activity, the geothermal heat rising from below the glacier can cause these cave systems to grow to considerable proportions. Such caves are found in the Cascade Arc in North America, the Vatnajökull glacier in Iceland, and the Perito Moreno glacier in Argentinian Patagonia.

Accessing and exploring these caves is difficult and dangerous. Glaciers are constantly moving and the cave roofs can collapse without warning. Because they are found high on mountainsides, mountaineering techniques are required to access them, and then caving equipment is needed to explore, and escape from, the caves themselves.

Sandy Glacier

Mount Hood is an active volcano in northern Oregon. Part of the volcanic Cascade Arc, it is home to 12 glaciers, one of which is the Sandy Glacier on the mountain's western slopes. Within the depths of the Sandy Glacier are the largest known glacier caves in the United States. However, because of the effects of global warming, Mount Hood's glaciers are retreating and the caves are becoming smaller every year.

GLOSSARY

AMA
Japanese pearl divers. Most ama are women.

ANTARCTIC CIRCLE
The area surrounding the South Pole, within which the sun remains under the horizon (in winter) or above the horizon (in summer) for a continuous 24-hour period.

AQUIFER
A layer of material below ground—either porous rock, gravel, sand, or silt—which can absorb water that has soaked down from the surface.

ARCTIC CIRCLE
The area surrounding the North Pole, within which the sun remains under the horizon (in winter) or above the horizon (in summer) for a continuous 24-hour period.

BLACK SMOKERS
A type of hydrothermal vent that releases dark black clouds of material. This is caused by sulfur compounds dissolved in the hot water, which precipitate back to solids when the water cools.

CARRACK
A multimasted sailing ship built from the thirteenth century onward.

CAVE DIVING
The exploration of water-filled caves undertaken with scuba-diving equipment.

CIRCLE OF LATITUDE
A continuous circle around Earth running in an east-west direction.
(Circles of longitude runs in north-south circles).

COURSE
The route taken by a river from its source to its mouth.

DEFORESTATION
Human activity that results in the destruction of the forest environment.

DENUDATION
A geological process in which the effects of the sun and wind cause Earth's surface to erode, breaking down rock formations and causing rocks and sand to slip down slopes.

DESERT PAVEMENT
A type of desert environment in which the desert floor is made up of small rock fragments and pebbles that have formed into a hard surface.

DISSOLUTION
The breakdown of limestone rocks by acidic water.

DIVING BELL
A metal chamber lowered from the side of a ship that lets occupants undertake work below the surface of the sea, for example, salvaging goods from a sunken shipwreck.

EXTREMOPHILES
Organisms that have evolved to survive in extreme conditions.

FLOWSTONE
Sheets of rock formed by minerals deposited by flowing water, usually within cave environments.

GALLEON
A multimasted sailing ship that evolved from the carrack. Galleons were built from the sixteenth century onward.

GLACIER CAVE
A cave formed within the ice of a glacier.

GLOBAL WARMING
The long-term rise in the average overall temperature of Earth's climate system, mainly caused by the release of greenhouse gases.

GREENHOUSE GAS
A gas that absorbs and releases heat energy, causing the surface of Earth to increase in temperature. Many greenhouse gases are produced by human activity.

GUIDELINE
A long length of rope secured to a cave entrance and towed by a cave diver, providing an easy-to-follow route back out of the cave.

HYDROTHERMAL VENT
An area of the seabed where volcanic activity causes seawater to become heated, sometimes to particularly high temperatures.

LAHARS
Fast-moving mudslides produced during some volcanic eruptions. Hot lava melts snow or ice on top of the volcano, causing large amounts of water to be suddenly released.

LAVA
Molten magma which has escaped through the Earth's crust during a volcanic eruption.

LAVA CAVE
A cave formed in volcanic rock as the result of the eruption of a volcano.

LONGSHIPS
Sturdy, ocean-going ships used by the Vikings for exploration, trading, and war. They were constructed from wood, with square cloth sails made from wool, and were powered both by sails and oars.

MAGMA
Fiercely hot molten rock within the Earth.

MICROCLIMATE
An small area with different climatic conditions to its surrounding area. For example, the cooler, shadier conditions found within a dense forest.

MOULIN
A shaft in the surface of a glacier, which can provide a route down into the glacier and, sometimes, to the area underneath.

MOUTH
The point at which a river flows into a larger body of water, either the sea or a lake.

OCEANOGRAPHY
The scientific study of the oceans.

OCEAN RIDGE
An underwater mountain system that has formed along the boundary of two tectonic plates on the ocean floor.

PALEO-ESKIMO PEOPLE
The earliest peoples who inhabited the Arctic regions and the ancestors of the Eskimo peoples.

POLES
The points on the surface of Earth through which the planet's axis of rotation extends.

PYROCLASTIC FLOWS
Fast-moving clouds of hot gases and rock fragments that are released during certain types of volcanic eruptions. They are extremely dangerous and destructive.

RIVER BASIN
The area of land where rainwater collects and flows into a river system.

SCUBA
Self-contained underwater breathing apparatus—a technology designed to let divers operate underwater without being connected to the surface with an air hose.

SPELEOGENESIS
The natural processes that result in the formation of caves.

SPELEOLOGY
The scientific study of cave environments.

STALACTITE
Long rock formations hanging from the ceiling, created by dripping water within cave environments.

STALAGMITE
Long rock formations rising from the floor, created by dripping water within cave environments.

TAIGA
A type of forest environment found across the most northerly countries on Earth, including Canada, Russia, Japan, Norway, Sweden, Finland, and Scotland. The trees present are mainly coniferous and include spruce, pine, and larch.

TECTONIC PLATES
The large sections of Earth's crust. The movement of these plates causes the formation of volcanoes, mountains, ocean trenches, and earthquakes.

THE BENDS
A dangerous condition, also known as decompression sickness, which occurs when a diver returns to the surface too quickly. This can cause gas bubbles to form within the diver's body, causing pain, headaches, and possibly death.

TREE CANOPY
The habitat contained within the sections of trees above the ground, from where the trunk emerges from the soil to the top of the tree.

TRIBUTARY
A river or stream that flows into another larger river or that flows into a lake, which then feeds a larger river.

TROGLOBITE
An animal species that has evolved to live entirely within an underground or cave environment.